The Principle of Position

BOOKS BY MILES J. STANFORD . . .

The Green Letters
The Ground of Growth
The Principle of Position
The Reckoning That Counts
Abide Above

Other Christian Classics . . .

All Through the Day by Guy H. O. King
Bone of His Bone by F. J. Huegel
Great Men of the Bible Volumes 1 and 2
　　by F. B. Meyer

Miles J. Stanford
The Principle of Position
Foundations of Spiritual Growth

ZONDERVAN PUBLISHING HOUSE
OF THE ZONDERVAN CORPORATION | GRAND RAPIDS, MICHIGAN 49506

THE PRINCIPLE OF POSITION
© 1976 by Miles J. Stanford

Library of Congress Cataloging in Publication Data
Stanford, Miles J
   The principle of position.
    1. Christian life—1960-   I. Title.
BV4501.2.S718   248'.4   75-46512
ISBN 0-310-33021-1

All rights reserved

Unless otherwise noted, the Scriptures quoted are taken from the American Standard Version of the Bible or the King James Version. All rights reserved. No portion of this book may be used in any form without the written permission of the publishers, with the exception of brief excerpts in magazine articles, reviews, etc.

Printed in the United States of America

83   84   85   86   87   88 — 10 9 8

CONTENTS

	Preface	7
1	Position Defined and Illustrated	9
2	Justification and Assurance	17
3	Reconciliation and Acceptance	23
4	Completeness and Security	30
5	Sanctification and Consecration	36
6	Identification and Growth	43
7	Sin and Purged Conscience	50
8	Sins and Conscience	57
9	Sins and Light	64
10	Sins and Confession	71

PREFACE

As the second in *The Green Letters* series, the dual purpose of this booklet is to help new Christians to start right, and older Christians to keep right.

The *positional* truths of the Word of God, which constitute the scriptural foundation of spiritual growth, are here set forth in correlated and concentrated form. Through Spirit-directed study of these chapters, we trust that each advancing believer may be firmly grounded in "the principles of the doctrine of Christ," and go on to maturity (Heb. 6:1).

"And it is my prayer that your love may be more and more accompanied by clear knowledge and keen perception for testing things that differ, so that you may be men of transparent character, and may be blameless, in preparation for the day of Christ, being filled with those fruits of righteousness which come through Jesus Christ—to the glory and praise of God" (Phil. 1:9-11, Wey.).

MILES J. STANFORD
Lakewood, Colorado

Chapter One

POSITION DEFINED AND ILLUSTRATED

The Principle of Position

All spiritual life and growth is based upon the principle of position. It can be summed up in one word: source.

Through physical birth we entered our human family position, from which source we derive certain characteristics. We are the product of our position. Just so in our spiritual birth. When we are born again, the risen Lord Jesus is the source of our Christian life; in Him we are positioned before our Father, in whom "we live, and move, and have our being" (Acts 17:28), "for we are His workmanship, created [born anew] in Christ Jesus" (Eph. 2:10). Our Father, in redeeming and recreating us, "raised us up with Him, and seated us with Him in the heavenly *places*, in Christ Jesus" (Eph. 2:6, ASV).

Our position, the source of our Christian life, is perfect. It is eternally established in the Father's presence. When we received the Lord Jesus as our personal Savior, the Holy Spirit caused us to be born into Him. He created us in the position that was established through His work at Calvary. "Therefore if any man be in

The Principle of Position

Christ, he is a new creature [creation]" (2 Cor. 5:17). This is the eternal position in which every believer has been placed, whether he is aware of it or not. The Christian who comes to see his position in the Lord Jesus begins to experience the benefit of all that he is in Him. His daily state is developed from the source of his eternal standing.

Our condition is what we are in our Christian walk, in which we develop from infancy to maturity. Although our position remains immutable, our condition is variable. Through the exercise of faith, our eternal position (source) affects our daily condition, but in no way does our condition affect that heavenly position. "If [since] ye then be risen with Christ, seek those things which are above, where Christ sitteth on the right hand of God" (Col. 3:1). "Be strong *in the Lord*—be empowered through your union with Him; draw your strength from Him" (Eph. 6:10, Amp.).

When we concentrate upon our condition, we are not living by faith but by feelings and appearances. The inevitable result is that we become increasingly self-conscious and self-centered. Our prime responsibility is to pay attention to the Lord Jesus, to rest (abide) in Him as our position. There will then be growth, and He will be more and more manifested in our condition. "But we all, with open face beholding as in a glass the glory of the Lord, are changed into the same image from glory to glory, even by the spirit of the Lord" (2 Cor. 3:18).

If the believer does not know of his position in the Lord Jesus, and how to abide in Him as his very life, there will be but one result. He will struggle in his un-Christlike condition rather than rest in his Christ-centered position.

In most cases, a believer is more aware of his condition than of his position. This is the reason for so much failure and stagnation. If we are to grow and become fruitful, our faith must be anchored in the finished work of our position—in Christ. There is no basis for faith in our changeable, unfinished condition.

Position Defined and Illustrated

". . . Your faith should not stand in the wisdom of men, but in the power of God" (1 Cor. 2:5).

Scriptural, fact-centered faith in the Lord Jesus as our position before the Father is the one means of experiencing that finished work in the growth of our daily condition. Spiritual birth placed us in our accepted position, from which our spiritual condition is being completed, by faith. ". . . Created in Christ Jesus unto good works, which God hath before ordained that we should walk in them" (Eph. 2:10).

Every Christian has been positioned forever in the risen Lord by spiritual birth. But only the believer who knows, grows. It is faith in the facts of our position that gives us the daily benefits of growth in our condition. If the believer is not clearly aware of the specific truths of the Word, he cannot exercise the necessary faith for growth and service. He can only seek his resources in the realm of self. Some of the wonderful positional truths are set forth for our faith in the scriptural illustrations of the grain of wheat, and the vine and the branch.

THE GRAIN OF WHEAT

In John 12:24 the Lord Jesus said, "Except a corn (grain) of wheat fall into the ground and die, it abideth alone: but if it die, it bringeth forth much fruit." This principle of life out of death was then established at Calvary's Cross, where He, as *the* Grain of Wheat, died and rose again. In His resurrection He brought forth the "much fruit" out of His death.

Everyone who would ever place his trust in Christ as Savior, every grain of wheat, was resident in (identified with) *the* Grain of Wheat, the Head of the new spiritual harvest. Every believer is included in the "much fruit" of His death and resurrection. "For if we have been planted together in the likeness of his death, we shall be also in the likeness of his resurrection" (Rom. 6:5).

The Principle of Position

THE PRINCIPLE OF REPRODUCTION

There is another wonderful principle involved here: *like produces like.* "And God said, Let the earth bring forth grass, the herb yielding seed, and the fruit tree yielding fruit *after his kind*" (Gen. 1:11, italics mine). Our Lord Jesus, as the Grain of Wheat having fallen into the ground in death, and having risen again unto life eternal, is still bringing forth the "much fruit," "after his kind." "For whom he [God] did foreknow, he also did predestinate to be conformed to the image of his Son, that he might be the *firstborn among many brethren*" (Rom. 8:29, italics mine). The Lord Jesus is our life; therefore, as we grow spiritually, the family likeness is manifested. We are gradually conformed to His image, who Himself is the "express image of his [God's] person" (Heb. 1:3). And, "when he shall appear, we shall be [completely] like him; for we shall see him as he is" (1 John 3:2).

In the natural realm, the first grain of wheat contained, complete and perfect, the life of every subsequent grain of wheat to this day. It did not abide alone, retaining all, but fell into the ground and died, finding resurrection in the "much fruit" of life out of death. This same principle applies in the spiritual realm. The position, the source of life, of every believer as a grain of wheat, is God's firstborn Grain of Wheat, our Lord Jesus Christ. Each of us is "after his kind"; we have His life. Thus, when we speak of our position, we refer to our place in the risen Lord—our "life is hid with Christ in God" (Col. 3:3).

The principle of position, therefore, both natural and spiritual, is that life in its fulness and completeness is resident in the source, and is transmitted through birth and growth. Resurrection life is explicitly after its kind; it is "conformed to the image" of its positional source. The Lord Jesus Christ as the Father's Grain of Wheat took our place at Calvary, and His death and resurrection brought forth the "much fruit" of similar grains of wheat, believers predestined to be conformed to the image of God's Son.

Position Defined and Illustrated

There is a stillness in the Christian's life:
  The grain of wheat must fall into the ground
And die; then, if it die, out of that death
  Life, fullest life, will blessedly abound.
It is a mystery no words can tell,
  But known to those who in this stillness rest;
Something divinely incomprehensible:
  That for my nothingness, I get God's best!
                                    —Selected

THE VINE AND THE BRANCH

Consistent with *the principle of position* and *the principle of reproduction,* our risen Lord Jesus is the Vine. As such, He brings forth fruit "after his kind." "I am the Vine, ye are the branches. He that abideth in me, and I in him, the same bringeth forth much fruit; for without me ye can do nothing" (John 15:5).

In the natural realm, the life that is already complete in the vine is increasingly supplied to the growing branches. The healthy condition of the branches is contingent upon their abiding in their position in the vine. The branch is not only a product and a living part of the vine, but that which is produced in the branch is also the fruit of the vine. Actually, the branch produces nothing, either for the vine, for others, or for itself. The vine, the positional source, has everything to do with the development and fruitfulness of all its branches. The chief responsibility of the branch is to rest just where it was born, to abide in its living position in its living source.

As the believer rests in his position, the life of the Vine (the "fruit of the Spirit") is manifested in his condition—"love, joy, peace, patience, kindness, goodness, faithfulness, gentleness, self-control" (Gal. 5:22, 23, NASB). The life of the Vine is the life of the branch. The True Vine is established at the right hand of our Father in glory and is the source from which our Christian life flows. The indwelling Spirit of Christ is the living link be-

The Principle of Position

tween Him in heaven and our spirit here on earth. ". . . He that is joined unto the Lord is one spirit" (1 Cor. 6:17).

Taking Our Position

We take our position, not by attempting to get into it, but simply by seeing that we are already positioned in the Lord Jesus. We abide in Him by resting in the fact. We have been in this risen position ever since our new birth. As we come to realize this truth and to "stand in our standing" in Him, we begin to experience the daily benefits of our life that is hid with Christ in God. Our attitude becomes, "I see my position in the Lord Jesus, and I abide there; I rest in Him, not only as my Savior, but as my life." Faith in our position will bring growth in our condition.

Paul prayed for believers, "That the God of our Lord Jesus Christ, the Father of glory, may give unto you the spirit of wisdom and revelation in the knowledge of him: the eyes of your understanding being enlightened; that ye may know what is the hope of his calling, and what the riches of the glory of his inheritance in the saints" (Eph. 1:17, 18). He also said, "Blessed be . . . God . . . who *hath* blessed us with every spiritual blessing in the heavenly places in Christ" (Eph. 1:3, ASV, italics mine).

Our Father intends us to know and understand that He has already provided, in Christ our life, everything required for our Christian life both in time and eternity. He is patiently teaching us to have no faith in the old man (self), and to exercise all of our faith in the new Man (Christ). We are told to do in faith what our Father has already done in fact. At the cross He freed us from the reign of sin and self; in the resurrection He united us to the risen Lord Jesus. By faith in the work of the cross, the old man is put off; by faith in our heavenly position in Christ, the new man is put on. Hence we are free to dwell within the very Source of every spiritual blessing with which our Father has blessed us.

Position Defined and Illustrated

By reckoning the old man to have been crucified at Calvary, he is "put off" daily (Rom. 6:11a). By reckoning ourselves as newly created in the risen Lord Jesus, we "put on" the new man (Rom. 6:11b). As we escape self's reign of death, we enter into Christ's reign of life.

1. PUT OFF THE OLD
   a. *Fact*
   "Knowing this, that our old man was crucified with him" (Rom. 6:6, ASV). ". . . seeing that ye have put off the old man" (Col. 3:9). Positionally, we were separated from the old Adamic nature in our identification with Christ on the cross.
   b. *Faith*
   "That ye put off concerning the former conversation (manner of life) the old man" (Eph. 4:22). By faith in our new, sanctified position, we turn from, we reckon as crucified, the principle of sin and self within. We count ourselves to be new creations in Christ, having died to sin and self. That is our part in putting off the old man that God put off from us at the cross.

2. PUT ON THE NEW
   a. *Fact*
   "For as many of you as have been baptized [spiritually] into Christ have put on Christ" (Gal. 3:27). "And have put on the new man, which is renewed in knowledge after the image of him that created him" (Col. 3:10). At our new birth we were recreated in Christ, and our Christian life is now hid with Him in God (Col. 3:3, 4).
   b. *Faith*
   "Put on the Lord Jesus Christ" (Rom. 13:14). ". . . Put on the new man, which after God is created in righteousness and true holiness" (Eph. 4:24). By faith in the positional

fact that our Father has placed us in His Son, we abide in Him, we acknowledge our place in Him. By faith, we stand in the position He has already given us. "Stand therefore, having your loins girt about with truth" (Eph. 6:14).

Chapter Two

JUSTIFICATION AND ASSURANCE

It may help us to see the importance of the principle of position in our Christian life if we consider the fact that God began training us in positional truth before we were born again!

JUSTIFICATION

According to His faithful ministry, the Holy Spirit brought about an initial conviction of sin by revealing our needy condition. Through varied pressures and circumstances, we came to realize our sinful state before God.

Then the Holy Spirit may have used a faithful witness to make clear to us from the Word that we were lost sinners, *positionally*. We were in the wrong family—we had been born into the fallen, sinful, condemned Adamic line. ". . . As in Adam all die" (1 Cor. 15:22). In our natural birth, we were born "dead in trespasses and sins" (Eph. 2:1). ". . . By one man's [Adam's] offence death reigned . . ." (Rom. 5:17).

In His perfect love and holiness, God made it possible for us to be removed from our position of death in Adam, and to be eternally born anew into His family through our position in the

The Principle of Position

Lord Jesus Christ. By His grace we were brought to turn from our natural, fallen condition and position, and to believe on His Son as our own personal Savior, our new position before God.

Much of this wonderful transaction and transition, no doubt, was not understood at the time. However, it is all-important that the truths of our new birth and justification become crystal clear if we are to experience the *benefits* of our position in Christ. Superficiality in this foundational step inevitably makes for shallowness and immaturity throughout our subsequent walk.

The meaning of justification is to pronounce righteous, not to make righteous; what is imputed is not, in fact, imparted. To be justified means that the believer is viewed in Christ as righteous, and is treated as such by God. The righteousness of our position in the Lord Jesus is increasingly manifested in our condition, as we "grow in grace, and in the knowledge of our Lord and Savior, Jesus Christ" (2 Pet. 3:18). "But of him are ye in Christ Jesus, who of God is made unto us . . . righteousness, and . . . redemption" (1 Cor. 1:30).

Until we clearly see the positional perfection of our justification in Christ, our conception of, and faith in, all the other aspects of our position will be out of focus. In Old Testament type, God explained to Israel that "the life of the flesh is in the blood: and I have given it to you upon the altar to make an atonement for your souls: for it is the blood that maketh an atonement for the soul" (Lev. 17:11). Now, the value of the life sacrificed is the measure of the worth of the blood shed. In that these type-sacrifices were animals, innocent and spotless though they were, still "it is not possible that the blood of bulls and of goats should take away sins" (Heb. 10:4). All this was a cancellation in anticipation of God's perfect sacrifice of "the Lamb of God, which taketh away the sin of the world" (John 1:29).

God the Son became also the perfect Son of Man in order that He might go to the Father's altar, the cross of Calvary, and there willingly shed His precious Blood in full atonement for our sins.

Complete payment made, He was free to rise again in resurrected, ascended, and glorified eternal life. "In whom we have redemption through his blood, the forgiveness of sins, according to the riches of his grace" (Eph. 1:7). There are two important factors in this verse: (1) "In whom we have redemption." Here we have our position of justification. When we received Him as our Savior, He received us and we were born into Him in "newness of life"—His life. (2) Because of the perfection of His atonement, it was all "according to the riches of his grace." Complete and eternal justification is a gracious *gift*, utterly impossible to be earned in any way whatsoever. ". . . To him that worketh not, but believeth on him that justifieth the ungodly, his faith is counted for righteousness" (Rom. 4:5).

A further fact to be remembered is that all of our sins were future at the time they were paid for, since the work of the Cross was accomplished when we were yet unborn. Our Father took everything into consideration before He made a single move on our behalf. Hence we can be fully assured that all our sins, past, present and future, have been forever forgiven. ". . . Through this Man is preached unto you the forgiveness of sins: and by him all that believe are justified from *all things*" . . . (Acts 13:38, 39, italics mine).

Since justification is in Christ and not in ourselves, it is a truth of position, not condition. We receive justification in the Lord Jesus by faith in the Word; it is a fact believed, not an experience received. It has nothing to do with our condition, but everything to do with our position. However, as we rest in our justified position, our spiritual condition is affected. We experience something of the new-found peace and joy of the Lord, and His love for us.

Assurance

The blessed assurance of salvation, and of justification in particular, is based squarely upon our position in the Lord Jesus as

The Principle of Position

our righteousness. Being non-experiential, justification can never be founded upon our condition. Assurance of justification results when we realize what our Father has done and said; it is never based on feelings. Someone has said, "Because God has spoken, I am *sure*; because I am sure, I *feel* at rest." "Set your mind on the things above, not on the things that are on earth" (Col. 3:2, NASB).

It is here that the first major mistake in our Christian life is often made. In taking the position of justification by faith in the Lord Jesus, this new standing of life began to make a marked difference in our state. Because of this, we shifted the basis of our assurance from eternal position to temporal condition. We looked, and felt, and sounded saved, hence we were assured of our salvation.

But then, one morning came the dawn! We didn't look very saved, we didn't feel at all saved, and so we didn't sound saved either. All day long everything and everybody went wrong, and by nightfall we found ourselves at the end of our assurance. Thoroughly shaken, we determined to rectify matters on the morrow. The next day we strove to look saved, to feel saved, and to sound saved. But, because we were centered in our condition, all was wretched failure. We even began to question our salvation. ". . . If the LORD be with us, why then is all this befallen us?" (Judg. 6:13).

In the Lord's time, the Comforter refocused our faith upon our position by means of the Word, and our assurance of salvation was again anchored upon the Rock, Christ Jesus. With this assurance reestablished, our condition began to improve as a result of the position in which we stood by faith. We had learned our first important lesson: the necessity of knowing and abiding in our position. Apart from this abiding, there is nothing but frustration and failure. "And the work of righteousness shall be peace; and the effect of righteousness quietness and assurance for ever" (Isa. 32:17).

Justification and Assurance

THE WITNESS OF THE SPIRIT

"The Spirit Himself [thus] testifies together with our own spirit, [assuring us] that we are children of God" (Rom. 8:16), Amp.). It is a temptation for many to hanker after something more tangible than the positional testimony of the Word, in order to be more sure of their assurance. But it is at this point that the faithful Spirit would teach us total reliance upon the Word, *nothing* added. " . . . Receive with meekness the engrafted word . . ." (James 1:21).

There may be other ground for assurance of our salvation, such as, "We know that we have passed from death unto life, because we love the brethren" (1 John 3:14), but this is secondary, not foundational. Besides, there will be times when our love for some brethren may falter, and then what of our assurance?

The witness of the Spirit is His witness to the Word wherein lies God's revelation of our eternal position. And in that Word He testifies concerning the Lord Jesus, who is our position before God. Although the Holy Spirit abides within and witnesses to our spirit, we must remember that the human spirit lies beyond the range of consciousness. Therefore, assurance of salvation is not gained through the senses. As we rest in our position by faith in the scriptural facts, the Spirit of truth gives us a deep, inexplicable assurance that cannot be altered. We not only believe, we *know*; our knowledge is established in the eternal, Spirit-ministered Scriptures. ". . . For I know whom I have believed, and am persuaded that he is able to keep that which I have committed unto him against that day" (2 Tim. 1:12).

All seems so simple and solved during the infant stage of our Christian life. But the Lord must take us on from milk to meat, to become responsible, spiritually intelligent, adult believers. We must not only become firmly and clearly established in the deeper truths ourselves, but we must be qualified to share them effectively with others. Once we are sure and sound, the Lord can establish others through us. But, "if the trumpet give an

The Principle of Position

uncertain sound, who shall prepare himself to the battle?" (1 Cor. 14:8).

Until we are solidly founded upon the first principles of spiritual birth, we cannot be taken on to the principles of growth and maturity. "For every one that useth milk is unskilled in the word of righteousness: for he is a babe. But strong meat belongeth to them that are of full age, even those who by reason of use have their senses exercised to discern both good and evil. Therefore leaving the principles of the doctrine of Christ, let us go on unto perfection [maturity]" (Heb. 5:13, 14; 6:1).

As the electronic eye of the space vehicle locks onto its designated star for guidance and maintenance upon its heavenly course, so are we to fix our eye of faith upon our heavenly position—the Bright and Morning Star. Thus, in our "looking unto Jesus the author and perfecter of our faith," we shall find experientially that "the path of the righteous is like the light of dawn, that shines brighter and brighter until the full day" (Heb. 12:2, ASV; Prov. 4:18, NASB).

Chapter Three

RECONCILIATION AND ACCEPTANCE

The settled assurance of our justification is not simply to make us sure of getting to heaven, but to prepare us for further spiritual progress. Assurance of our justified position in Christ gives us sureness in each subsequent step of our spiritual development. By grace we were born anew: "Being justified freely by his grace . . . " (Rom. 3:24); and by grace we will grow: "But grow in grace . . ." (2 Pet. 3:18). We must stand in the first principles before we can go on from them to maturity. Until we rest assured in our position of justification, we are not spiritually prepared for the positional truths of our reconciliation to, and acceptance by, God.

RECONCILIATION

The ground of our reconciliation to God is justification from the penalty of sin. In the Lord Jesus we were justified from the death penalty of sin, thereby enabling God to reconcile us to Himself. Justification frees us *from death*; reconciliation brings us *into life*. "For if while we were enemies we were reconciled to God

The Principle of Position

through the death of His Son, it is much more [certain], now that we are reconciled, that we shall be saved [daily delivered from sin's dominion] through His [resurrection] life" (Rom. 5:10, Amp.).

To be reconciled is to be brought into right relationship, into harmony. Being dead in our sins, we were completely cut off from any relationship with the God of life; spiritually, we were the children of the devil (John 8:44). Instead of seeking to bring to life and reconcile the fallen Adamic nature—an impossibility, because that life is enmity toward God and cannot be subject to the law of God (Rom. 8:7)—our Father recreated us in the life of the Lord Jesus. He placed us in a totally new position, out of Adam, into Christ. "Even when we were dead . . . He made us alive together in fellowship and in union with Christ. He gave us the very life of Christ Himself, the same new life with which He quickened Him" (Eph. 2:5, Amp.).

Self cannot be reconciled to God. Since we were born sinners and therefore were enmity against God, our reconciliation to Him was no simple matter. It took the cross of Calvary to solve the problem. There, as lost and alienated sinners, we were identified with the Lord Jesus in His death unto sin and resurrection unto God; we were raised from the dead as new creatures (creations) in Christ (2 Cor. 5:17). Being made "partakers of the divine nature" (2 Pet. 1:4), we were completely and eternally reconciled to the Father. "Having made peace through the blood of his cross, by him to reconcile all things unto himself. . . . And you, that were sometime alienated and enemies in your mind by wicked works, yet now hath he reconciled in the body of his flesh *through death,* to present you holy and unblameable and unreproveable in his sight" (Col. 1:20-22, italics mine).

Our present condition is infinitely inferior to our eternal position, but our Father accepts us—not in ourselves, but in His Son. Our Lord Jesus so completely justified us in His death and resurrection that our Father is absolutely just in eternally reconciling us. His love and life are free to flow. "For he hath made him to be sin for us, who knew no sin; that we might be made the righteousness of God in him" (2 Cor. 5:21). ". . . All things are from God, Who through *Jesus* Christ reconciled us to Himself (received us into favor, brought us into harmony with Himself)" (2 Cor. 5:18, Amp.). Due to His work of justification and reconciliation, there is full acceptance for us.

ACCEPTANCE

Here we have one of the most vital positional subjects, and yet it is relatively unknown among believers today. All too few are enjoying the benefits of acceptance in their daily walk. The believer who is not aware of his position of acceptance *in Christ* is caught in the struggle to improve his condition in order to feel acceptable to God. But the believer who abides in the Lord Jesus as his righteousness and acceptance is freed from futile self-effort. Standing in his position, he trusts Christ to manifest Himself increasingly in his life. He is free from the burden of himself and has become burdened on behalf of others. God "hath given to us the ministry of reconciliation" (2 Cor. 5:18).

CONDITION

First of all, we must consider the area in which we are not accepted by God, nor ever can be. It is only natural for us to feel that our spiritual walk and service make us acceptable to our Father. We imagine that it is our responsibility (with His help) to live and serve so faithfully and fruitfully that He will approve of us, and therefore continually and abundantly bless us. We are making the natural mistake of depending upon condition, instead of position, for our acceptance.

Important as it is, service is often a condition-centered detriment in the lives of many zealous believers. When service is given predominance over fellowship with and growth in the Lord Jesus, *doing,* instead of *being,* takes over in the life. Fellowship

The Principle of Position

and growth must ever take precedence over service and activity, otherwise spiritual declension sets in.

In this reversal of God's order for us, the heart seeks satisfaction and a sense of acceptance through production (law), instead of reception (grace). Bible study and prayer, as well as one's outlook, become almost exclusively service-centered. Instead of life bringing forth service, service becomes the life. Thus, as long as the service goes well, the servant is happy and feels accepted. But once the service wanes, or fails to produce results, all else falls with it. We are to be sons, not servants. "Wherefore thou art no more a servant, but a son . . ." (Gal. 4:7).

In time, we begin to realize that there is something very wrong with this entire concept. We become aware that our walk and service are less and less acceptable, even to ourselves. In seeking to *do* rather than to *be*, in attempting to give out more than we take in, our condition becomes barren and carnal. We have been depending upon self to do what only Christ our life can do; the farther we move on this tangent, the more active and malignant the self-life appears to be.

What the condition-centered believer does not realize is that God Himself is causing this shattering revelation of self. He takes us into situations and relationships that finally cause us to face up to the fact of our failure as Christians—our nothingness, our total unacceptability in ourselves. Not until we understand that in our flesh there "dwelleth no good thing" (Rom. 7:18), can we rest in our position of complete acceptance in the Lord Jesus, just as we are. To abide in Christ, and to consent to be loved while unworthy, is the believer's positional privilege and responsibility. Love functions according to its nature, not according to the quality of its object.

The believer who is not abiding by faith in the acceptable One, but who is relying upon his personal condition for acceptance, is hopelessly handicapped in the matter of fellowship, growth and service. He is entangled in the self-effort of working to improve his condition, and is inevitably cast down in utter defeat. How can a defeated, depressed, self-centered Christian enjoy fellowship with the Father, or be at peace with Him? Yet, devastating as this Romans Seven trek is, it is our Father's preparation of us in order that we may shift our reliance and faith from our condition in ourselves, to our position in Christ. ". . . Not I, but Christ . . ." (Gal. 2:20).

POSITION

"Having predestinated us unto the adoption of children by Jesus Christ to himself, according to the good pleasure of his will, to the praise of the glory of his grace, wherein he hath made us *accepted in the beloved*. In whom we have redemption through his blood, the forgiveness of sins, according to the riches of his grace" (Eph. 1:5-7, italics mine). In learning to take our position in the Lord Jesus and thereby to abide in Him as our acceptance, we grow to expect less and less from ourselves, and more and more from Him. "My soul, wait thou only upon God; for my expectation is from him" (Ps. 62:5).

As we become more fully established in our position, we are increasingly willing to reject self, to leave all that sinful source on the cross for daily crucifixion. This progressive freedom from the dominion of self gives us a deepening rest in the Lord Jesus; we become rooted and grounded in the Source of life, where we grow effortlessly and fruit is borne to His glory. Self-effort produces the works of the flesh (Gal. 5:19-21), while positional rest fosters the fruit of the Spirit (Gal. 5:22, 23).

"Abide in me [your position], and I in you. As the branch cannot bear fruit of itself, except it abide in the vine; no more can ye, except ye abide in me. I am the vine, ye are the branches: He that abideth in me, and I in him, the same bringeth forth much fruit: for without me ye can do nothing" (John 15:4, 5). Although we abide in the Lord Jesus as our position, we are ever aware of our condition in ourselves. We are concerned about the

The Principle of Position

sinfulness of self, but no longer do we depend upon improvement in that realm for our acceptance. We are resting in a position, in a Person who is fully and forever accepted by God, One in whom there is no improvement necessary or possible. We have exchanged unimproveable self for the perfect One.

Established in our position, we become increasingly aware of our acceptance in Him and are more free to fellowship with our Father. In this blessed communion we grow, becoming more manifestly conformed to His image. ". . . We all, with open face beholding as in a glass the glory of the Lord, are changed into the same image from glory to glory, even as by the Spirit of the Lord" (2 Cor. 3:18). We are basically Christ-centered, instead of self-centered. Through our position in Him we have peace, joy and fellowship which abide all along our cross-centered path as our spiritual condition is developed.

One of the foremost benefits of resting in our position of acceptance is the deep and undying assurance that God is *for* us. "For I know the thoughts that I think toward you, saith the Lord, thoughts of peace, and not of evil, to give you an expected end" (Jer. 29:11). ". . . Having made peace through the blood of his cross . . ." (Col. 1:20). "There is therefore now no condemnation to them which are in Christ Jesus. . . . If God be for us, who can be against us?" (Rom. 8:1, 31).

As the Holy Spirit applies the finished work of the cross to the sinful source within, this inner crucifixion may lead us to think God is against us. But it is just the opposite; everything He takes us through is for our spiritual growth. ". . . *All* things work together for good to them that love God, to them who are the called according to his purpose. For whom he did foreknow, he also did predestinate to be conformed to the image of his Son . . ." (Rom. 8:28, 29). Therefore, "in everything give thanks: for this is the will of God in Christ Jesus concerning you" (1 Thess. 5:18). "He that spared not his own Son, but delivered him up for us all, how shall he not with him also freely give us all things?" (Rom. 8:32). "For all things are for your sakes, that the abundant grace might through the thanksgiving of many redound to the glory of God" (2 Cor. 4:15).

What a safe and impregnable position is ours in Christ! "The Lord is my rock, and my fortress, and my deliverer; my God, my strength, in whom I will trust; my buckler, and the horn of my salvation, and my high tower" (Ps. 18:2). When the "accuser of the brethren" points his maligning finger at the self-life within, at our condition in ourselves, seeking to get us to question our acceptance, we are able to rest in our position and point to Christ. We are well aware of self's unacceptability, but we are much more aware of our acceptance in the Beloved. The enemy can never touch Him, and our "life is hid with Christ in God" (Col. 3:3). Satan may be the counsel for the prosecution, but we have two Counsels for defense—an Advocate at the throne, and an Advocate within—to say nothing of the fact that the righteous Judge is our Father!

"Wherefore in all things it behoved him to be made like unto his brethren, that he might be a merciful and faithful high priest in things pertaining to God, to make reconciliation for the sins of the people" (Heb. 2:17). Our Father has reconciled us to Himself in a way that enables Him to be consistent with Himself, being both "just, and the justifier of him which believeth in Jesus" (Rom. 3:26).

Chapter Four

COMPLETENESS AND SECURITY

Each faith-step we take concerning the facts of our position prepares us for the following one, since every succeeding step is established upon all that precedes. Our faith grows by feeding upon properly related scriptural truth. "For precept must be upon precept . . . line upon line . . ." (Isa. 28:10). "The steps of a good man are ordered by the Lord . . ." (Ps. 37:23).

Many hungry-hearted believers are struggling to get into the experience of Romans Eight when they are not yet resting in the facts of Romans Three. They feel guilty because they fall far short of the heights of Ephesians and Colossians, when in fact they do not adequately know peace with God in Romans Five, to say nothing of identification with Christ in Romans Six. The experience of Romans Seven is well known, however. It is absolutely necessary to allow the Holy Spirit to take us along in God's sequence of Scripture, as each plane of truth is foundational for the next. Skip over one, and firm footing for the next is lost. "Hold up my goings in thy paths, that my footsteps slip not" (Ps. 17:5).

Completeness and Security

COMPLETE IN HIM

Once we are scripturally assured of our justification, reconciliation, and acceptance in the Lord Jesus, we are to feed upon the truth of our completeness in Him. "As ye have therefore received Christ Jesus the Lord [by faith], so walk ye in him: rooted and built up in him, and stablished in the faith, as ye have been taught, abounding therein with thanksgiving. . . . For in him dwelleth all the fulness of the Godhead bodily. And ye are complete in him . . ." (Col. 2:6, 7, 9, 10).

All we will ever need for our Christian life, now and forever, is ready and waiting in the Lord Jesus, complete and accessible. Our condition is absolutely dependent upon our completed Source. Faith rests upon our Father's scriptural testimony as to what He has already done for and with us in Christ, never upon what He is doing for and with us in our present condition. Faith in the Vine brings forth fruit in the branches.

Resting in our position in the Lord Jesus has a direct effect upon our condition. When we know that our Father has already made us complete in Christ, we are able to trust Him in the midst of His development of that completeness in our spiritual condition. Without the knowledge of this finished work in the Lord Jesus, our faith lacks the necessary confidence that He will make sure progress in our daily growth.

Think for a moment of the positional truth of 2 Corinthians 5:17, ". . . If any man be in Christ, he is a new creature [creation]: old things are passed away; behold, all things are become new." In the Lord Jesus we are altogether new creations, born anew and complete in Him. He is the eternal Source from which our condition is to develop. "For we are God's [own] handiwork (His workmanship), recreated in Christ Jesus, [born anew] that we may do those good works which God predestined (planned beforehand) for us, (taking paths which He prepared ahead of time) that we should walk in them—living the good life which He prearranged and made ready for us to live" (Eph. 2:10, Amp.).

The Principle of Position

Even though the work is complete in Christ, there is nothing automatic about our experience of it. Ours is the responsibility of faith. We were not only born anew by faith, but we are to live, walk, and grow by faith. To enter intelligently and cooperatively into that which our Father has established for us in Christ, by faith we are to "put on the new man, which after God is created in righteousness and true holiness" (Eph. 4:24). This simply means that we are to rest in our position in the Lord Jesus as our life. We are to abide there because we have already been established (born) there. "And have put on the new man, which is renewed in knowledge after the image of him that created him" (Col. 3:10). "For as many of you as have been baptized [spiritually, by the Holy Spirit] into Christ have put on Christ" (Gal. 3:27).

"But put ye on the Lord Jesus Christ, and make not provision for the flesh, to fulfill the lusts thereof" (Rom. 13:14). The Lord Jesus is "put on" as we abide *in* Him by faith. Our risen Lord is full provision for our Christian life and service; and the cross is the only provision we have for the self-life. As we confidently rest in the Lord Jesus, the Holy Spirit gives us the things of Christ by means of growth. As a result, our condition begins to reflect what we already are in position. By faith, we abide and live in Him; by faith, His life is developed and manifested in us. "My little children, of whom I travail in birth again until Christ be formed in you" (Gal. 4:19).

Secure in Christ

Based upon the preceding facts, the eternal security of the believer becomes a foregone conclusion; once the Holy Spirit establishes the Christian in the previous steps, there can be no question about this one. But without the required scriptural preparation, there is bound to be a nagging question mark hovering in the background: am I unconditionally and forever saved, or am I on probation?

The secure believer may now and then be accosted by those

who strongly oppose any thought of unconditional, eternal security. They refer to it as "that damnable doctrine," and insist that such a belief results in lawlessness. What these dear people fail to grasp is that the believer who truly stands in the grace of positional security is the one who most fully fears God and hates sin. And he hates sin for what it is, not just for its consequences. Moreover, his is not a slavish fear; it is not a fear of losing God's love, but of offending and grieving it.

"But there is forgiveness with thee, that thou mayest be feared" (Ps. 130:4). The fear of the secure believer is a reverential trust, coupled with hatred of evil. "The fear of the Lord is to hate evil . . ." (Prov. 8:13). "For the grace of God that bringeth salvation hath appeared to all men, teaching us that, denying ungodliness and worldly lusts, we should live soberly, righteously, and godly, in this present world" (Titus 2:11, 12). Grace banishes all guesswork, and gives one assurance; the law keeps one guessing.

The truth of security holds the Christian firm in the midst of the process of growth. It is the insecure believer who is naturally unstable and flounders from one "experience" to another, never learning and therefore never arriving at the truth. Resting in our eternal position frees us from the futile and sinful self-effort of trying to make our condition the basis of our security. Abiding in our eternal security in Christ gives the steadiness of faith necessary for the Holy Spirit to carry on His gracious ministry within—that of dealing with self in crucifixion, and thereby causing us to "grow in *grace*, and in the knowledge of our Lord and Saviour Jesus Christ" (2 Pet. 3:18).

The spiritual explanation for opposition to true eternal security is not the claim that it produces lawlessness. It is rather that those who oppose do not exercise faith in the Word, which would enable them to see and accept their position in the risen Lord for assurance, acceptance and security. They are condition-centered, hence self-centered and earthbound.

The Principle of Position

On the other hand, the believer who knows he has died unto sin and has been recreated in the risen Lord Jesus, understands that he has no other position before God than the very life of Christ. "For ye are all the children of God by faith in Christ Jesus" (Gal. 3:26). "And if children, then heirs; heirs of God, and joint-heirs with Christ . . ." (Rom. 8:17). "Beloved, now are we the sons of God, and it doth not yet appear what we shall be: but we know that, when he shall appear, we shall be like him . . ." (1 John 3:2).

It certainly is not yet manifest in our condition what we already are in our position, or what we shall be when He appears. But the resting believer does not rely upon appearances, neither is he affected one way or another by his condition. He knows he is accepted and secure on a different basis altogether, that of his position in Christ, the Man of God's choosing. This is not carelessness, but confidence in Him. In quietness and assurance we are to continue, "waiting for the coming of our Lord Jesus Christ: who shall also confirm you unto the end, that ye may be blameless in the day of our Lord Jesus Christ" (1 Cor. 1:7, 8).

The believer who rests in the *Son of God* knows he is eternally secure. "For you have died and your life is hidden with Christ in God. When Christ, who is our life, is revealed, then you also will be revealed with him in glory" (Col. 3:3, 4, NASB). "And not only so, but we also joy in God through our Lord Jesus Christ, by whom we have now received the atonement" (Rom. 5:11).

The believer who rests in the *sovereignty of God* knows he is eternally secure. "For whom he did foreknow, he also did predestinate to be conformed to the image of his Son, that he might be the firstborn among many brethren. Moreover whom he did predestinate, them he also called: and whom he called, them he also justified: and whom he justified, them he also glorified" (Rom. 8:29, 30). "Now unto him that is able to keep you from falling, and to present you faultless before the presence of his glory with exceeding joy . . ." (Jude 24).

Completeness and Security

The believer who rests in the *justice of God* knows he is eternally secure. "To declare . . . his righteousness: that he might be just, and the justifier of him which believeth in Jesus" (Rom. 3:26). "For Christ also hath once suffered for sins, the just for the unjust, that he might bring us to God . . ." (1 Pet. 3:18). "There is therefore now no condemnation for those who are in Christ Jesus. For the law of the Spirit of life in Christ Jesus has set you free from the law of sin and of death" (Rom. 8:1, 2, NASB).

The believer who rests in the *will of God* knows that he is eternally secure. "Ye have not chosen me, but I have chosen you, and ordained you, that ye should go and bring forth fruit, and that your fruit should remain . . ." (John 15:16). "But of Him are ye in Christ Jesus, who of God is made unto us . . . redemption" (1 Cor. 1:30).

The believer who rests in the *love of God* knows he is eternally secure. ". . . I have loved thee with an everlasting love: therefore with lovingkindness have I drawn thee" (Jer. 31:3). "Who shall separate us from the love of Christ? shall tribulation, or distress, or persecution . . . ? . . . For I am persuaded, that neither death, nor life, nor angels, nor principalities, nor powers, nor things present, nor things to come, nor height, nor depth, nor any other creature, shall be able to separate us from the love of God, which is in Christ Jesus our Lord" (Rom. 8:35, 38, 39).

Chapter Five

SANCTIFICATION AND CONSECRATION

There need be no difficulty with the subject of sanctification once the meaning of the term is understood. In both the Hebrew and the Greek, sanctification is synonymous with separation. To be sanctified means to be "set apart" for God's possession and use.

It is important to realize that the term has nothing whatsoever to do with the thought of cleansing or purification, as so many seem to think. For example, it is recorded that, prior to the advent of sin into the world, "God blessed the seventh day, and sanctified it" (Gen. 2:3). He set apart the Sabbath as a special day. Further, the sinless Lord Jesus said, "I sanctify myself" (John 17:19). He willingly set Himself apart, He separated Himself, He completely devoted Himself to the work the Father gave Him to do.

Position

It is all-important to keep in mind the clear scriptural distinction between our fully-sanctified position and our being-sanctified condition. Positionally, our Father has already done the work on our behalf, just as He has already justified, reconciled, accepted, and secured us—in the Lord Jesus. Note the difference between the Corinthians' position, and their condition: (1) "Unto the church of God which is at Corinth, to them that are sanctified in Christ Jesus, called to be saints, with all that in every place call upon the name of Jesus Christ our Lord . . ." (1 Cor. 1:2); (2) "For it hath been declared unto me of you, my brethren . . . that there are contentions among you" (1 Cor. 1:11).

In the first place, it is heartening to realize that our sanctification is both *the will, and the work, of God*. "For this is the will of God, even your sanctification . . ." (1 Thess. 4:3). "And the very God of peace sanctify you wholly. . . . Faithful is he that calleth you, who also will do it" (1 Thess. 5:23, 24). He has sanctified us positionally because we looked to Him for salvation; He will sanctify us experientially as we look to Him for growth.

Every believer, whether babe or veteran, is already separated unto God in Christ Jesus. What makes the difference in the believer's condition is that he becomes clearly aware of his sanctified position in the risen Lord. Jude wrote his epistle "to them that are sanctified by God the Father, and preserved in Jesus Christ, and called" (v. 1). Our Father has eternally set us apart and preserved us in His Son, and called us to His service. All of the growing believer's life is considered service, whether it be formal or otherwise.

Our sanctification is not only the will and the work of the Father, but it is *in and through the Son*. "But of him are ye in Christ Jesus, who of God is made unto us . . . sanctification . . ." (1 Cor. 1:30). Here we can see that our positional sanctification is a gift, just as is our righteousness. When through faith we were born into the Lord Jesus, *He* became our righteousness and our sanctification, not partially, but completely. "For in him dwelleth all the fulness of the Godhead bodily. And ye are complete in him . . ." (Col. 2:9, 10).

The Principle of Position

It is a great relief and joy for the struggling believer to realize that when he received Christ as his righteousness by faith, he also received Him as his sanctification. Many people struggle and work for a righteousness of their own, until they finally receive His righteousness by faith. Then, as believers, they set about to labor through the whole futile process again, struggling to produce a sanctification of their own instead of resting in His sanctification as a gift. The Lord Jesus sent Paul unto the Gentiles "to open their eyes . . . that they may receive forgiveness of sins and an inheritance among those who have been sanctified by faith in Me" (Acts 26:18, NASB).

As is everything else in our position in Christ, our sanctification is perfect, once for all, complete, eternal. It could not be otherwise, since the Lord Jesus Himself is our sanctification. Hebrews 10:10 and 14 leave no question about this wonderful fact: "By the which will we are sanctified through the offering of the body of Jesus Christ once for all. . . . For by one offering he hath perfected forever them that are sanctified." Through the cross of the Lord Jesus Christ, and in His life, our Father has created us anew and given us a completely separated position before Himself—separated from all that would hinder that blessed relationship. "Therefore if any man be in Christ, he is a new creature [creation]: old things are passed away; behold, all things are become new" (2 Cor. 5:17). "I know that, whatsoever God doeth, it shall be forever: nothing can be put to it, nor any thing taken from it: and God doeth it . . . " (Eccl. 3:14).

CONDITION

As we abide in our position of sanctification, there is growth in our condition of sanctification. Although the Holy Spirit participated in establishing our positional sanctification—"But you were washed, but you were sanctified . . . in the name of the Lord Jesus Christ, and in the Spirit of our God" (1 Cor. 6:11, NASB)—He is mainly concerned with our condition of sancti-

Sanctification and Consecration

fication. He it is who brings us into experiential separation unto our Father. Peter wrote his first epistle to the "elect according to the foreknowledge of God the Father, through sanctification of the Spirit" (1 Peter 1:2).

Truth is the basis upon which the Holy Spirit carries out His ministry. He is the Spirit of truth, the truth of the Scriptures (John 16:13). ". . . God hath from the beginning chosen you to salvation through sanctification of the Spirit and belief of the truth" (2 Thess. 2:13). The Lord Jesus prayed to the Father, "Sanctify them through thy truth: thy word is truth" (John 17:17).

It is by means of the Spirit-ministered Word that we see and understand the facts concerning our position of sanctification in the Lord Jesus. Without the scriptural facts, there would be nothing upon which we could base our faith. But as we see that the Holy Spirit has already sanctified us in Christ, we are able to trust Him to separate us unto God in our condition. The Spirit carries out His *subjective work* in our lives from the basis, the source, the standing, the position, the *objective truth*, of our eternal completeness in our risen Lord Jesus Christ.

In this matter of faith in the Word, it is essential to distinguish between God's *promises* and His *facts*. Promises are to be anticipated; facts are to be accepted. We wait upon our Father to fulfil His promises in His own time, according to His will and His integrity. On the other hand, facts are to be appropriated and enjoyed now; we are to accept them with thanksgiving.

By faith we know that we are justified (Rom. 5:1), that we are reconciled (Col. 1:20-22), that we are accepted (Eph. 1:5-7), and that we are sanctified (Acts 26:18). Since the Holy Spirit ministers to us through the channel of faith, He gives us in our condition what we appropriate from our position. For instance, in the matter of peace, from our position of justification we receive peace concerning the penalty of our sins; from our reconciliation, peace with God; from our acceptance, the peace of

The Principle of Position

God; and from our sanctification, peace and assurance that He will conform us to the image of our Lord Jesus.

CONSECRATION

Without a clear understanding of our position of sanctification, there can be no valid consecration. To dedicate, to separate, to consecrate ourselves unto God is simply our response of faith to the separation, the sanctification in which God has already placed us. It is acknowledging our position of sanctification. Consecration does not call upon us to do anything, but to rest in what God has already done. Unless we know that we have been sanctified in the Lord Jesus, we cannot respond in consecration to Him.

PSEUDO CONSECRATION

Why does so much sincere consecration come to nought? The main reason is that most well-meaning Christians seek to consecrate to God that which He has totally and forever rejected. Not yet understanding their position of sanctification as new creations in Christ, they consecrate *self* to God in the hope that the "old man" will become spiritual and thus usable in His service.

The believer must learn by two means the fact that the self-life is unimprovable. (1) Specific Scripture: God never intends to improve the old man, because "the natural man receiveth not the things of the Spirit of God . . . neither can he know them, because they are spiritually discerned" (1 Cor. 2:14). Further, "the flesh lusteth against the Spirit, and the Spirit against the flesh: and these are contrary the one to the other" (Gal. 5:17). Everything of the first Adam is unalterably opposed to everything of the Last Adam. Self is implacable in its attitude toward God, having the very essence of the Enemy. "Because the carnal mind is enmity against God: for it is not subject to the law of God, neither indeed can be" (Rom. 8:7). (2) Personal experience:

Sanctification and Consecration

One's daily life proves beyond a doubt that the sinful Adamic source within never changes. The awakened and honest believer must admit that self is as capable of sin after fifty years of the Christian life as it was before he was saved—sometimes, it seems, even more so!

No, our Father can accept nothing of the Adamic life, no matter how "good" or "religious" it may seem in the natural realm. And when the believer sees that God has taken all the old life to the cross and crucified it with Christ, he will likewise count (reckon) it crucified, and take his place of consecration as alive unto God in Christ Jesus.

SCRIPTURAL CONSECRATION

True, acceptable, abiding consecration is expressed most clearly in Romans 6:13, "Neither yield ye your members as instruments of unrighteousness unto sin: but yield yourselves unto God, as those that are alive from the dead, and your members as instruments of righteousness unto God." Here we have the key statement in Scripture concerning consecration: "*as those that are alive from the dead.*" We know that the old man did not rise from the dead. The wages of sin is death, and the sinful Adamic life was condemned and crucified in Christ on the cross (Rom. 6:6). But the recreated life, the new man in Christ Jesus, arose from the dead in His resurrection. ". . . you were also raised up with Him through faith in the working of God, who raised Him from the dead. And when you were dead in your transgressions and the uncircumcision of your flesh, He made you alive together with Him . . ." (Col. 2:12, 13, NASB).

It is this new life, our Christian life, the life that is already hid with Christ in God, that we are to yield, to consecrate, to set apart unto our Father. It is the only acceptable life—the life that He has already accepted in His beloved Son. In consecration we are carrying out our responsibility of responding to that which He has already done, of willing according to His will, of gladly

The Principle of Position

yielding to Him that which already belongs to Him. In the matter of *life,* it is "yield yourselves unto God . . . and your members as instruments of righteousness" (Rom. 6:13). In the matter of *service,* it is "present your bodies a living sacrifice, holy, acceptable" (Rom. 12:1).

Consecration is based upon reckoning (Rom. 6:11). We turn *from* the old man by counting ourselves to have died unto sin and self. We turn *to* our position in the risen Lord by counting ourselves as new creations alive unto God in Christ Jesus. Abide above!

Chapter Six

IDENTIFICATION AND GROWTH

Positional truth is the basis of every sphere of our Christian life. But nowhere are we more dependent upon the principle of position than in the understanding of our identification with the Lord Jesus in His death unto sin and resurrection unto God. As in all positional steps, identification is not experiential, but is a matter of placing our faith in the facts of the Word. Whereas justification has to do with *birth*, identification has to do with *growth*, which is to continue until we see Him face to face.

Position

When we received the Lord Jesus as our Savior and thus were born into Him as our life, all that He *is* and all that He *has* became ours. Justification (His righteousness) was perhaps all that we could apprehend at the time, but that was only the beginning of an infinity of wonders into which we are to enter, now and throughout eternity. Because of our grace-given position in the Heir, we are "heirs of God, and joint-heirs with Christ" (Rom. 8:17).

All is held in trust for us in Christ, our new position, and

The Principle of Position

becomes our condition as we are taken forward, step by step, in faith. When we are able to receive and appreciate the benefits of the riches of Romans chapters One through Five, then He is free to take us into the reality of the wealth of Romans chapters Six through Eight. When we are firmly established in the positional truth of Christ dying *for* our sins and rising again for our justification (Rom. 4:25), then we are prepared to see our position and enter into the benefits of our having died and risen *with* Him (Rom. 6:5).

Now, let us look at some of the positional truths concerning our identification with the Lord Jesus. "For if we have become united with him in the likeness of his death, certainly we shall be also in the likeness of his resurrection" (Rom. 6:5, NASB). For us to be reborn, newly created in the risen life of the Savior, God had to free us from the penalty of sin and the nature of the fallen Adam. He accomplished this by placing us in Christ on the cross, by identifying each one of us, as future believers, with Him. Thus, when Christ died *unto* sin (out of the realm and reign of the principle of sin), we as sinners died unto sin in Him. Why should this be so difficult to comprehend when we understand clearly that the Lord Jesus died for every one of our sins (all future at the time) on that same cross? He was identified with our sin in order that we might become identified with His righteousness. "For he hath made him to be sin for us, who knew no sin; that we might be made the righteousness of God in him" (2 Cor. 5:21).

We know that the Lord Jesus rose again, once He had paid in full the wages of sin. Since we were identified with Him in His death, and thereby were freed from both the penalty and power of sin, we know that we arose with Him in His resurrection. It could not be otherwise. "Now if we have died with Christ, we believe that we shall also live with Him" (Rom. 6:8, NASB).

"For the death that He died, He died to sin, once for all; but the life that He lives, He lives to God" (Rom. 6:10, NASB). The Lord Jesus died unto the power and reign of sin, and He rose

Identification and Growth

again in the "power of an endless life" (Heb. 7:16). Identified with Him on the cross, we too died unto sin's tyrannical dominion and "have been buried with Him through [spiritual] baptism into death: in order that as Christ was raised from the dead through the glory of the Father, so we too might walk in newness of life" (Rom. 6:4, NASB).

God provides the facts before He calls for faith. Early in Romans Six we are asked, "Know ye not" that all who were identified with the Lord Jesus were identified in His death (v. 3)? In verse 6 Paul says, "Knowing this, that our old man was crucified with Him" (Rom. 6:6, ASV). It is not until the facts of our identification with Christ are understood that we are admonished to exercise faith. In this way there is no effort or struggle to reckon, because we *know*.

Yes, it is in the clear light of our identification with Christ in His death and resurrection that we are directed to "reckon ye also yourselves to be dead to sin, but alive to God in Christ Jesus" (Rom. 6:11, ASV). It would be utterly impossible for our Father even to suggest that we count ourselves as having died unto sin and become alive unto Him in Jesus if it were not already true of us! Nor could He ever call upon us to consecrate ourselves to Him "as alive from the dead" (Rom. 6:13) if He had not already made us "new creations" in the risen Christ (2 Cor. 5:17).

However, true as our identification with the Lord Jesus is, if we are not fully aware of the facts we will derive little benefit from them in our daily life. And that is where we need them. Moreover, unless we realize our need of the separating (sanctifying) power of our death and life in Him, there will be no motivation for our faith to reach out and receive. To reckon upon a positional fact is to see it clearly, to believe it, to count upon it, to receive and appropriate the practical reality of it with thanksgiving. "Rooted and built up in him, and stablished in the faith, as ye have been taught, abounding therein with thanksgiving" (Col. 2:7).

The Principle of Position

> Death and judgment are behind us,
> Grace and glory are before;
> All the billows rolled o'er Jesus,
> There they spent their utmost power.
>
> Jesus died, and we died with Him,
> Buried in His grave we lay,
> One with Him in resurrection,
> Now "in Him" in Heaven's bright day.

The gracious Spirit of truth revealed to us that the Lord Jesus died for our sins, and by faith in the facts we entered into the position of justification (which included our complete and eternal salvation). When the Holy Spirit reveals to us the truth of our Lord Jesus having died unto sin, and our identification with Him in that death and resurrection, by faith in the facts we acknowledge our position—we reckon ourselves to have died unto sin and to be forever alive unto God in Christ.

That which we reckon in our position becomes experiential in our condition. As we count ourselves to have died unto sin on the cross, the effect of that cross is applied by the Spirit to the sinful self-life. "For we which live are alway delivered unto death for Jesus' sake . . ." (2 Cor. 4:11). Self is crucified, held in the place of death, as we are led into sacrificial paths for His glory. As self is thus dealt with by the cross, our condition reflects progressively the facts of our position in Christ. ". . . That the life also of Jesus might be made manifest in our mortal flesh" (2 Cor. 4:11).

CONDITION

"But God be thanked, that ye were the servants of sin, but ye have obeyed from the heart that form of doctrine which was delivered you. Being then made free from [the power of] sin, ye became the servants of righteousness" (Rom. 6:17, 18). Our daily experience can be no more true than the doctrine we hold, and by which we are held.

Identification and Growth

The steps would be as follows: (1) We finally see and understand our *position*, our identification with Christ in having died unto the dominion of sin and been made alive unto God in Him. (2) We become aware of the need to be separated in our *condition* from self and unto Christ. (3) We then exercise faith in the completed work of our *position* by reckoning upon the facts of our death and resurrection in Christ. (4) On the basis of this faith, the Holy Spirit is free to translate the truth of our position into our daily condition.

The Spirit of Christ is extremely practical in His operations. He uses everyday means in bringing our positional sanctification into our experience. As we reckon upon the fact of self's crucifixion, He conveys the effect of that finished work into our lives through daily circumstances. Due to our weakness and sinfulness, He is able to utilize situations and human relationships to show us what we are in ourselves. We are thereby faced with the choice: self, or Christ. If we count ourselves to have died unto sin and self, the emancipation of the cross is experienced within. And as we abide in the Lord Jesus, knowing ourselves to be alive unto God in Him, He is free to manifest Himself more fully in our condition. This is spiritual growth. The "works" of the flesh are curtailed, the "fruit" of the Spirit is revealed. "For to me to live is Christ . . ." (Phil. 1:21).

". . . Unless a grain of wheat falls into the earth and dies, it remains by itself alone; but if it dies, it bears much fruit" (John 12:24, NASB). This statement of the principle of life out of death applies primarily to the Lord Jesus Christ. He is the Grain of Wheat who refused to abide alone as God's only begotten Son, but gave Himself at Calvary to become the "firstborn among many brethren" (Rom. 8:29). Since He died and rose again, thereby bringing forth "much fruit," and that harvest being after His kind, our lives as similar grains of wheat are based upon the same principle of life out of death.

No matter how self-contained and comfortable our Christian

The Principle of Position

life may be, there is bound to develop a deep heart-hunger to see others become grains of wheat. The Lord Jesus "shall see his seed . . . He shall see of the travail of his soul, and shall be satisfied" (Isa. 53:10, 11). His heart-hunger is expressed through Paul: "My little children, of whom I travail in birth again until Christ be formed in you" (Gal. 4:19). And the Spirit of Christ yearns in our hearts that the Lord Jesus may gain a rich and lasting harvest of golden grain through us.

This entire life-out-of-death process is directly related to our reckoning upon our position of life out of death. As we yearn to be used, to multiply, to be brought to harvest, the Holy Spirit takes us down into death in our experience. He "plants" or "buries" us in this difficult situation or that dark area and, as the old life is thus held in the place of death (inoperative), the new life grows up and is manifested not only in us, but in others through us. "So then death worketh in us, but life in you [others]" (2 Cor. 4:12).

Conversely, when we are self-centered and refuse the path of the cross, we think little of others and everything of ourselves. We scheme, fight, maneuver, and even pray to "abide alone." But the Lord Jesus has established the principle that "whosoever will save his life shall lose it [no fruit, no harvest]: but whosoever will lose his life for my sake ['alway delivered unto death for Jesus' sake'], the same shall save it [shall see it multiplied and harvested in others]" (Luke 9:24).

Actually, the Holy Spirit patiently uses everything (and everyone) in His process of bringing us to the grain-of-wheat stage. When we are self-centered and carnal, He applies the appropriate pressures—perhaps in the physical body, the home, or the place of work—thereby, in time, causing us to hunger to be Christ-centered.

When we begin to see and hate the self-life for what it is, when we begin to see and love the Lord Jesus for who He is, then it is we become willing for the Holy Spirit to take self into death

Identification and Growth

in order that Christ may be formed in us. "We are assured and know that [God being a partner in their labor], all things work together and are [fitting into a plan] for good to those who love God and are called according to [His] design and purpose. For those whom He foreknew—of whom He was aware and loved beforehand—He also destined from the beginning (foreordaining them) to be molded into the image of His Son [and share inwardly His likeness], that He might become the first-born among many brethren" (Rom. 8:28, 29, Amp.).

Chapter Seven

SIN AND PURGED CONSCIENCE

Briefly, it can be said that due to the fall man came into possession of a moral sense to distinguish right and wrong, known as conscience. Man's sinful condition, however, renders conscience an unreliable guide. Nevertheless, the Holy Spirit works upon the conscience in bringing conviction of sin.

THE NATURAL MAN

Due to such factors as heredity, social and religious training, and environment, the conscience of the unbeliever has an erratic range all the way from good to very bad. But either way, its ground of reference is wrong since it is centered in the self-life. ". . . When they measure themselves with themselves and compare themselves with one another, they are without understanding and behave unwisely" (2 Cor. 10:12, Amp.). At best, the unsaved are under legal bondage; ". . . they are a law to themselves. . . . They show that the essential requirements of the Law are written in their hearts and are operating there; with which their conscience (sense of right and wrong) also bears witness . . ." (Rom. 2:14, 15, Amp.).

Even when the unbeliever's conscience is clear, this state is often attained by a combination of rationalization and good works, resulting in self-righteousness. Hence his so-called good conscience is the very element that tends to keep him from seeing his need for God's righteousness and life. On the other hand, when his conscience is bad, he flees from God with a sense of despair because of personal unworthiness. It is only when the Holy Spirit convicts the mind, heart, and conscience concerning sin, whether of self-righteousness or of unworthiness, that the sinner can see his need of turning to Christ.

THE CARNAL MAN

As far as his conscience is concerned, the carnal Christian is much the same as the unbeliever. By dint of self-effort to produce some good works for God, and the blind rationalization of comparing himself with supposedly weaker Christians, he is able sporadically to maintain some semblance of a good conscience. This very feeling, false as it is, tends to exaggerate his dependence upon himself. "But he that glorieth, let him glory in the Lord. For not he that commendeth himself is approved, but whom the Lord commendeth" (2 Cor. 10:17, 18).

When the carnal believer's conscience is bad, he seeks to hide from God, and even attempts to place the blame for his sinfulness upon others. Yet, the Holy Spirit often works through the conscience to turn such a one to the Lord Jesus for cleansing from unrighteousness and for spiritual growth. "Let us all come forward and draw near with true (honest and sincere) hearts in unqualified assurance and absolute conviction engendered by faith [that is, by that leaning of the entire human personality on God in absolute trust and confidence in His power, wisdom and goodness], having our hearts sprinkled and purified from a guilty (evil) conscience . . ." (Heb. 10:22, Amp.).

The Principle of Position

THE SPIRITUAL MAN

The believer who rests in his position rather than his condition, who abides in his risen Lord in the presence of the Father, is growing spiritually. He is fully assured that "Christ also hath once suffered for sins, the just for the unjust, that He might *bring us to God*" (1 Pet. 3:18, italics mine). By simple faith in the facts, he acknowledges his place in Christ who is his life, the One who, "when he had by himself purged our sins, sat down on the right hand of the Majesty on high" (Heb. 1:3). Knowing his sins to be purged once for all, his conscience is thereby clear, since "the worshippers once purged" have "no more conscience of sins" (Heb. 10:2).

The spiritually minded believer is conscious of sin *in* him, but he is fully assured that there is no sin *on* him; all of his sin has been laid upon the Lord Jesus. Although his condition is needy, for he is indwelt by the principle of sin, he *lives* in his position in Christ. His constant resources for spiritual growth are received from on high. He knows his freedom to "come boldly unto the throne of grace" in order that he may "obtain mercy, and find grace to help in time of need" (Heb. 4:16).

When the growing believer sins, his conscience and his communion with the Father being thereby disturbed, he freely confesses his sin. He knows that the Lord Jesus "is faithful and just to forgive us our sins, and to cleanse us from all unrighteousness" (1 John 1:9). He also has recourse to the truth that when he does sin he has "an advocate with the Father, Jesus Christ the righteous" (1 John 2:1). Hence a pure conscience and communion are restored and maintained, and he is free to continue his fellowship with the Father and the Son. He has learned that "if we walk in the light . . . we have fellowship one with another, and the blood of Jesus Christ his Son cleanseth us from all sin" (1 John 1:7).

CONDITION

The condition-centered Christian has no other recourse but to fight against indwelling sin, and thus seek to control self as best

Sin and Purged Conscience

he can. Added to this intolerable burden is the frustrating fact that God does not seem to help him in this endeavor. He is immersed in the defeat of Romans Seven. He battles here below, only to lose; he should rest above, where he is sure to win.

One of the chief reasons so many believers are spiritually ill (as well as mentally and physically) is a guilty, oppressed conscience. They are laboring under the burden of their unrighteous condition, rather than resting in the liberty of their righteous position. Sad to say, there aren't many of God's people today who know anything at all about a "pure," a "perfect," conscience. Countless Christians, including those who are awakened and hungry to grow, are bound by a bad conscience. They are honestly aware of their sinful condition, but are only vaguely aware of their perfect position.

This chapter has to do with the basic reason for the guilty conscience, which is the indwelling principle of sin. The next chapter will deal with the product of that principle, sins committed. First the cause, then the effect. There is a tremendous paradox in the Christian who, although redeemed by the Lord Jesus Christ from the penalty and tyranny of sin, nevertheless is rendered spiritually helpless and useless by an overwhelming burden of guilt.

We are thinking of the hungry-hearted Christian who is awakened to the sin of self, since he is the only one who is ready (prepared by the Holy Spirit) to be freed from this guilty condition. Awareness of need is the primary motivation for intelligent faith. Is this not the cry of the honest, struggling, guilt-ridden believer?: ". . . I do not understand my own actions—I am baffled, bewildered. I do not practice or accomplish what I wish, but I do the very thing that I loathe [which my moral instinct condemns] . . . . However, it is no longer I who do the deed, but the sin [principle] which is at home in me and has possession of me" (Rom. 7:15, 17, Amp.). Here is the progressing believer who sees his condition, but not as yet his position.

The Principle of Position

POSITION

There is but one place in which faith can rest, and that is in our Lord Jesus, where the Father has positioned us. And it is only in that abiding place that our conscience can be clear with regard to indwelling sin. Our guilt cannot be relieved through removal of the sin within, because that principle will be present as long as we reside in our unredeemed body. Nor is there hope of relief through improvement of self, since in the flesh there dwells no good thing to improve.

There was also the problem of a guilty conscience prior to Calvary. Then, into the holy place made with hands "went the high priest alone once every year, not without blood, which he offered for himself, and for the errors of the people . . . which was a figure for the time then present, in which were offered both gifts and sacrifices, that could not make him that did the service perfect, as pertaining to the *conscience*. . . . But Christ being come an high priest . . . by a greater and more perfect tabernacle, not made with hands . . . neither by the blood of goats and calves, but by his own blood he entered in once into the holy place, having obtained eternal redemption for us" (Heb. 9:7, 9, 11, 12).

Yes, our Lord Jesus "appeared to put away sin by the sacrifice of himself" (Heb. 9:26). ". . . We are sanctified through the offering of the body of Jesus Christ once for all. . . . But this man, after he had offered one sacrifice for sins for ever, sat down on the right hand of God. . . . For by one offering he hath perfected for ever them that are sanctified" (Heb. 10:10, 12, 14). As new creations in Christ Jesus, we have been redeemed from the penalty of indwelling sin; further, we have been sanctified (separated) from the domination of that same principle of sin. We have sin in us, but not on us; always indwelling, but never imputed!

It is essential to know how definitely and thoroughly God dealt with this principle of sin, especially since its presence within us is

Sin and Purged Conscience

so burdensome. ". . . God sending his own Son in the likeness of sinful flesh, and for sin, condemned sin in the flesh" (Rom. 8:3). The principle of sin has not been forgiven, it has not been cleansed; neither has it been improved, nor removed. But, thanks be unto God it has been condemned by the crucifixion of the cross. In His flesh, our Lord Jesus condemned the sin in our flesh. Thus condemned, there can now be no condemnation for us.

"There is therefore now no condemnation to them which are in Christ Jesus. . . . For the law of the Spirit of life in Christ Jesus hath made me free from the law of sin and death" (Rom. 8:1,2). It is due to this blessed fact that our conscience finds peace, and is purged from the guilt of indwelling sin.

It should not be difficult for us to make the correct choice between the consciousness of our condition, and the revelation of our position. If, because of feelings and lack of scriptural knowledge, we put more stock in our condition than our position, we will continue to labor under the intolerable burden of a defiled conscience. But if we agree with God concerning His condemnation of the old man, there is a perfectly peaceful conscience for us in the matter of indwelling sin. It is the infinite difference between our telling Him what we are in ourselves (condition), or heeding His testimony as to what we are in His Son (position). The former means guilt and enslavement, the latter freedom and growth.

At Calvary, when our Lord Jesus was made to be sin for us, He was crucified and thereby sin was condemned. At the same time, He took each potential believer as a sinner down into that death. Then he brought us up out of death, as new creations, in His resurrection life. Now and forever, the only position we have as believers is before our Father in His risen Son, cut off (sanctified) from our old relationship to indwelling sin by our death and resurrection in Him.

Once for all, the Lord Jesus has separated us in death and

The Principle of Position

resurrection from both the guilt and the power of indwelling sin. "But now once at the consummation of the ages He has been manifested to put away sin by the sacrifice of Himself" (Heb. 9:26, NASB). "For both he that sanctifieth and they who are sanctified are all of one . . ." (Heb. 2:11). Resting in this position not only purges our conscience from all guilt concerning the self-life, but also gives us increasing freedom from its domination.

Why not acknowledge and thank Him for this wonderful position, purchased at infinite price and so freely given? Anything we do short of resting in Him as our position, anything we attempt to do beyond that rest, is to slight the perfection of His life and work. "For you have died and your life is hidden with Christ in God" (Col. 3:3, NASB). "How much more shall the blood of Christ, who through the eternal Spirit offered himself without spot to God, purge your *conscience* from dead works to serve the living God?" (Heb. 9:14 italics mine).

Chapter Eight

SINS AND CONSCIENCE

"We have been sanctified through the offering of the body of Jesus Christ once for all" (Heb. 10:10, ASV). It is because of His work on the cross that our conscience is at peace despite indwelling sin. Once we know our conscience to be purged concerning the ever-present principle of sin, we can rest in our Father's gracious provision for the sins we commit—but not until. The fact of sin within can in no way keep us from resting and rejoicing in our risen Lord, abiding in the very presence of our Father. He Himself, after condemning sin in the flesh, "raised us up with Him, and seated us with Him in the heavenly places, in Christ Jesus" (Eph. 2:6, NASB).

Advocate

When we are at rest concerning sin, through abiding in the risen Lord, we are established and ready to receive His answer to the problem of *sins committed*. There are two factors that come into play when we have sinned: Christ's advocacy (this chapter); our confession (next chapter). His advocacy is the foundation for our confession.

The Principle of Position

"My little children, these things write I unto you, that ye sin not. And if any man sin, we have an advocate with the Father, Jesus Christ the righteous" (1 John 2:1). An advocate is one who speaks in support of another. Our Lord Jesus has entered heaven, "now to appear in the presence of God for us" (Heb. 9:24). As our High Priest, He is in God's presence on our behalf; He is there as our propitiation, our atonement.

"But this man, after he had offered one sacrifice for sins for ever, sat down on the right hand of God" (Heb. 10:12). He is seated because, as far as our acceptance and position before God are concerned, there is nothing more required either to do, or say. ". . . By his own blood he entered in once into the holy place, having obtained eternal redemption for us" (Heb. 9:12).

As our Advocate, the Lord Jesus is before the Father, maintaining us in fellowship with Him. There, in our position, we are "perfected forever" (Heb. 10:14). Here, in our condition, indwelt by the principle of sin, we are often overcome by its power. Nevertheless, by the ministry of the Spirit our condition is being perfected, or matured.

When we sin in word, thought or deed, consciously or unconsciously, our heavenly Advocate speaks to the Father on our behalf. His faithful intercession is justly founded upon His perfect work and Person, and thereby our right of position in our Father's presence is forever maintained. Although our sins are never imputed to us, they do defile us and hinder our fellowship with the Father.

Even though God fully and justly accepts the atonement of His Son on our behalf, He in no way passes over or tolerates our sins. He has not only provided His Son as our Savior, but also as our Advocate. "If any man sin, we have an advocate with the Father, Jesus Christ the righteous" (1 John 2:1). Further, He has given us the responsibility and privilege of confessing our sins. ". . . He that is washed [atonement] needeth not save to wash his feet [confession] . . ." (John 13:10). For, "if we confess our sins, he is faithful and just to forgive us our sins, and to cleanse us from all unrighteousness" (1 John 1:9).

Not only do we have an Advocate in heaven before the Father, but we also have an Advocate within our spirit. The word "Comforter" in John 14:16 is rendered "advocate" in 1 John 2:1. We need, and have, a dual advocacy! When we sin, Jesus intercedes for us on the ground of His having borne the judgment of that very sin. The indwelling Spirit acts upon our conscience to produce confession. Thereby we have the assurance of the sin having been forgiven, the unrighteousness cleansed, and our fellowship with the Father completely restored.

"So too the (Holy) Spirit comes to our aid and bears us up in our weakness; for we do not know what prayer to offer nor how to offer it worthily as we ought, but the Spirit Himself goes to meet our supplication and pleads in our behalf with unspeakable yearnings and groanings too deep for utterance. And He Who searches the hearts of men knows what is in the mind of the (Holy) Spirit—what His intent is—because the Spirit intercedes and pleads [before God] in behalf of the saints according to and in harmony with God's will" (Rom. 8:26, 27, Amp.). "He restoreth my soul: he leadeth me in the paths of righteousness for his name's sake" (Ps. 23:3).

The fact that we need constant advocacy before our Father in no way detracts from the truth of our perfect and eternal standing in the Lord Jesus. The Word makes it clear that each of us, at the moment of our new birth, is fully accepted in the Beloved. We are complete in Him, perfectly and forever forgiven, justified sanctified, and glorified—through His death, resurrection and ascension—never to come into judgment, but have passed from death to life as new creations in Christ Jesus. Before God, we are not in the flesh (the fallen, first Adam race), but in the Spirit (the new, Last Adam creation). Having died unto sin, self, Satan, the law, and the world, we are now and forever alive in our risen Lord "after the power of an endless life" (Heb. 7:16).

The Principle of Position

CONDITION

Although we are not in the flesh as to our position, we are in the body pertaining to our condition. While we are complete in Christ who is our life, as new creations in Him we have to be matured in the midst of the pressures and exigencies of everyday experience. Moreover, all is carried on in this "body of death" which is indwelt by the principle of sin. Therefore, we need the two faithful Advocates who undertake to fulfil God's purpose in and through us, despite the power of the world, the flesh and the devil.

The negative and positive aspects of our spiritual growth could be summarized in these words: (1) We are to reckon ourselves to have died unto sin, thus giving the Holy Spirit freedom to apply the finished work of the Cross to indwelling sin, so that it may be progressively held inoperative. (2) At the same time, we are to reckon ourselves (as new creations) alive unto God in Christ Jesus, abiding in Him as a branch in the True Vine.

Praise the Lord that, if and when we do sin in thought, word or deed, consciously or otherwise, "we have an advocate with the Father, Jesus Christ the righteous: and he is the propitiation for our sins" (1 John 2:1, 2). His advocacy has nothing whatsoever to do with our eternal standing, nor is it the placating of an angry, vengeful God (He already bore the wrath due our sin). But in His personal reconciliation on the cross and righteous presence before God, He makes it possible for our Father justly to show us mercy despite our sins.

The chasm between our perfect position and our imperfect condition is bridged by His advocacy and cleansing. Our only source of life and growth is in Christ. From that completed source our condition is gradually developed. Our progress on earth is dependent upon our fellowship with Him in heaven. Because of sins committed, that fellowship must be restored by Christ's advocacy and our confession. As we mature spiritually, there are fewer sins to be confessed. How futile to seek to deal with sins in any

Sins and Conscience

other way than through His advocacy and our confession!

There are those who, for one reason or another, by-pass the identification truths of Romans Six, and rely rather upon confession and cleansing for dealing with the problem of sin. But there is no real spiritual progress unless the source of sins is dealt with continually by the Spirit's application of the cross. He carries on that ministry as we reckon upon self having been crucified. Apart from this, there is nothing but the endless struggle of the treadmill—sinning, repenting, confessing, but then sinning again and again. On this erroneous basis there is no dealing with the source that relentlessly produces the sins.

Rather, we are to learn to rely upon the cross to deal with the sin principle, as we abide in the risen Lord for our spiritual growth. Then, if we do sin, we depend upon our Advocate in heaven to reestablish our fellowship with the Father, and our Advocate within to repair the spiritual damage by means of conviction, leading us to repentance and confession.

While living in this world it is heartening to realize that we neither have to ask nor to plead for His intercession. Both our Advocates are unceasingly interceding for us. "Wherefore he is able also to save them to the uttermost that come unto God by him, seeing he ever liveth to make intercession for them" (Heb. 7:25). The fact that we commit sins despite such faithful ministry does not reflect upon the worth or effectiveness of the intercession, but upon *our* faithfulness. We fail to count upon our death unto sin and our life in Christ.

If it were not for the constant intercession of our heavenly Advocate, our faith would surely fail when we are overcome, or when we willingly submit to the tyranny of sin and self. Think of what happened when Simon Peter denied his Lord: ". . . Simon, Simon, behold, Satan hath desired to have you, that he may sift you as wheat; but I have prayed for thee, that thy faith fail not: and when thou art converted [restored], strengthen thy brethren" (Luke 22:31, 32).

The Principle of Position

The Lord Jesus did not pray that Peter might not sin, but, having fallen, that his faith would respond to His Lord's advocacy. His faithful intercession kept Peter from self-centered despair, giving him grace for true repentance, deep sorrow for his sin, purity of conscience, and restoration of fellowship.

POSITION

At rest in our position in the Lord Jesus, we can depend upon the Holy Spirit to take us through all that is required for our growth in the purpose of God. "Inasmuch, then, as we have in Jesus, the Son of God, a great High Priest who has passed into Heaven itself, let us hold firmly to our profession [confession] of faith. For we have not a High Priest who is unable to feel for us in our weaknesses, but one who was tempted in every respect just as we are tempted, and yet did not sin. Therefore let us come boldly to the throne of grace, that we may receive mercy and find grace to help us in our times of need" (Heb. 4:14-16, Wey.).

We must face the fact that there is going to be constant need, even as we are more fully learning to hate (reject) self and love the Lord Jesus. In that God is "just, and the justifier of him which believeth in Jesus" (Rom. 3:26), He is free to utilize even our failures as He develops our condition. ". . . All things work *together* for good to them that love God . . ." (Rom. 8:28). In all that we go through we are taught more fully to reject self via the cross, and to abide in Christ via our position. At the same time, we are to count more upon His advocacy and rejoice in the privilege of our fellowship with the Father. Moreover, we thus become better fitted to understand and minister to our weaker brethren, knowing full well what they are going through. ". . . When thou art converted [restored], strengthen thy brethren" (Luke 22:32).

If we turn from our position of rest to fight against sin, and work to improve our condition, we have stepped off the rock of grace into the swamp of self-effort. But as we turn from self to abide in our Lord at the right hand of the Father, we find that He has dealt with both the principle of sin, and our sins.

We can rest in the fact that His work of atonement is never repeated, as His Word assures us: " 'And their sins and offences I will remember no longer.' But where these have been forgiven no further offering for sin is required" (Heb. 10:17, 18, Wey.). We depend upon the fact that His work as Advocate is never interrupted, "seeing he ever liveth to make intercession for them" (Heb. 7:25).

"Since therefore, brethren, we have confidence to enter the holy place by the blood of Jesus, by a new and living way which He inaugurated for us through the veil, that is, His flesh, and since we have a great priest over the house of God, let us draw near with a sincere heart in full assurance of faith, having our hearts sprinkled clean from an evil conscience . . ." (Heb. 10:19-22, NASB).

Chapter Nine

SINS AND LIGHT

"But if we [really] are living and walking in the Light as He [Himself] is in the Light, we have [true, unbroken] fellowship with one another, and the blood of Jesus Christ His Son cleanses (removes) us from all sin and guilt . . ." (1 John 1:7, Amp.).

What is this light in which we have been placed, in which we are to live and walk? "And this is the message . . . which we have heard from Him and now are reporting to you: God is Light and there is no darkness in Him at all—no, not in any way" (1 John 1:5, Amp.). Since our Father is Light, our Lord Jesus is Light also. "For God, who commanded the light to shine out of darkness, hath shined in our hearts, to give the light of the knowledge of the glory of God in the face of Jesus Christ" (2 Cor. 4:6).

While here on earth, the Lord Jesus said, "I am the light of the world" (John 8:12). Nevertheless, the full extent of that light was kept almost totally obscured by His humanity. For a brief moment, while on the Mount of Transfiguration, He allowed the true light within to be manifested. "And [He] was transfigured before them: and his face did shine as the sun, and his raiment was white as the light" (Matt. 17:2). Peter wrote later that he

Sins and Light

and the others "were eyewitnesses of His majesty" (2 Pet. 1:16). At present, our Lord Jesus is in glory, "on the right hand of the Majesty on high" (Heb. 1:3). It is in His light that we are to abide and walk, for "now are ye light in the Lord: walk as children of light" (Eph. 5:8).

Every Christian is positionally in the light, but until he learns to abide and walk in that light he can only struggle on in the darkness of sin and self. "For once you were darkness, but now you are light in the Lord. . . . For the fruit—the effect, the product—of the Light . . . [consists] in every form of kindly goodness, uprightness of heart and trueness of life" (Eph. 5:8,9, Amp.). Our blood-bought position is in the light of our Father's presence.

CONDITION

The healthy babe in Christ begins well, whether or not he knows anything at all concerning his position in the light. Being a child spiritually, he is handled as such by the Father. He feels that the Lord Jesus is very close to him and is leading him by the hand. He is filled with the joy of the Lord, and loves Him with all his heart. Although he is looking to the Lord Jesus, he is still self-centered because of ignorance regarding his position in Him. He is taken up mainly with what Christ has done, is doing, and will do *for him*; he is, in turn, seeking to live and work *for* the Lord. For the most part, he is emotionally motivated and therefore affected by his condition rather than his position.

Later, during the believer's spiritual adolescence, the Lord begins His reversal of all this. The emphasis in the life is to be shifted from dwelling on what Jesus Christ has done to rejoicing in who, what and where He is; from being happy and active, to being like Him; from living and working for Christ, to living in and working through Him; from what the believer is in himself, to what he is in Christ and what He is in the believer. From condition to position—"not I, but Christ."

The Principle of Position

Of necessity, the transitional process from a condition-centered to a position-centered life is extremely painful. "Now no chastening [child-training] for the present seemeth to be joyous, but grievous: nevertheless afterward it yieldeth the peaceable fruit of righteousness unto them which are exercised thereby" (Heb. 12:11). "For whom the Lord loveth he chasteneth . . ." (Heb. 12:6).

In spite of the believer's good beginning, and in the midst of his joy and activity for the Lord, self begins to creep back into the picture. The indwelling principle of sin once more asserts its tyrannical power, and the world regains its attraction. Peace and love tend to weaken and drain away. The "quiet time" quietly dies. Study of the Word becomes burdensome work. The conscience is defiled; sins are no longer confessed, but excused. The eyes are off the Lord, the struggle with self is on—simply because condition has been given precedence over position.

Now the faltering believer becomes keenly aware of self, and only vaguely aware of the Son. Desperately upset about his failing condition, he struggles to improve himself, all the while begging God to give him relief and "victory." This is the vantage point Satan has been waiting for. He slyly leads the believer to compare the present condition with the happy, carefree days gone by, and to question every realm of belief, thus shaking all reliance upon the Word and the Lord. He ruthlessly puts the wavering Christian on the defensive in every aspect of his life and walk. He applies downward pressure, and fills the heart with the gnawing remorse of self-condemnation.

When the believer allows the Enemy to spread the choking smog of self-accusation over his life, the realization of his righteousness in Christ is dimmed. The goal of Satan is to lure the believer back onto the ground of condemnation, in order to negate the benefits of his resurrection with Christ and his union with Him in the heavenlies.

Those who are not established upon the "no condemnation"

ground of Romans 8:1 make very little spiritual progress. They go just so far and then bog down; their fruit falls before it ripens. But the destroying power of the Enemy is rendered null and void when the believer rests in the truth that "the law of the Spirit of life in Christ Jesus hath made me free from the law of sin and death" (Rom. 8:2).

Although the Holy Spirit, as Convicter, puts the heart in an agony of conviction of sins, He never points downward. While Satan's accusation results in self-consciousness, Holy Spirit conviction leads to Christ-consciousness. When He convicts the heart and conscience concerning sins, He leads the believer to the self-judgment of confession. He then points upward to the remedy for sins committed—the blood that has opened the way to the peace and life of our position in the light of God's presence. "Having therefore, brethren, boldness to enter into the holiest by the blood of Jesus" (Heb. 10:19).

The Enemy spurs the failing one to self-effort by holding the impossible standard of perfection over the very imperfect believer's head. He agitates continually for immediate and complete rectification of the failing condition. But the patient Holy Spirit, on the other hand, allows time for development, graciously reminding of the ever-available and finished work of the shed blood for our cleansing from all unrighteousness throughout the process of growth. He gently leads the faltering believer from self-centeredness and darkness to Christ-centeredness and light. To bring this about, the Spirit of truth presents positional truth: "If [since] ye then be risen with Christ, seek those things which are above, where Christ sitteth on the right hand of God" (Col. 3:1). "For you have died and your life is hidden with Christ in God" (Col. 3:3, NASB).

Position

The awakened Christian who is not resting in his position becomes discouraged by his condition. Therefore, confession of

The Principle of Position

his sins is sporadic and he has little or no assurance of being cleansed from all unrighteousness. He is out of fellowship with the Father and the Son, and finds himself convicted by the Holy Spirit whom he is grieving. He is also under the domination of sin and self, as well as the condemnation of the devil. He is utterly wretched, with his sins accumulated as a cloud obscuring the light of his position of freedom and fellowship in his risen Lord.

But it is the history of Satan always to overstep himself. His most apparent victories all contain the seed of his own defeat. The very need generated by the believer's failure is the Spirit's preparation for his seeing and abiding in his blessed position of light. His faith is to be focused upon the fact that God has already given him a position in His presence; what is more, He has already established him in that position! "I have blotted out, as a thick cloud, thy transgressions, and, as a cloud, thy sins: return unto me; for I have redeemed thee" (Isa. 44:22).

The honest but still self-centered believer is oppressed and hindered by the darkness of his sinful condition. Nevertheless, in the midst of his downward trend, the Holy Spirit is presenting the truth so as to overwhelm him by the light of his righteous position. "And ye shall know the truth, and the truth shall make you free" (John 8:32). Not only is he free from the penalty of sin, but also from its power to bring forth sins. The believer is bound until, in spite of his sins, he rests in the truth concerning those sins.

What, then, is the specific truth concerning our sins? In our condition, we are totally unacceptable for the Father's presence and fellowship. But position is what counts with God, and it must come first with us! "Giving thanks unto the Father, which *hath* made us meet [suitable] to be partakers of the inheritance of the saints in light: who *hath* delivered us from the power of darkness, and hath translated us into the kingdom of his dear Son: in whom we *have* redemption through his blood, even the

Sins and Light

forgiveness of sins" (Col. 1:12-14, italics mine). ". . . The blood of Jesus Christ his Son cleanseth us from all sin" (1 John 1:7).

Every believer, regardless of his present condition, is in the very presence of the Father; we are in Christ, at the right hand of the Majesty on high. The source of our Christian life is in the light above, in Christ risen. It is there we are to abide; it is that completed standing which alone will affect the growth of our daily state. "And, having made peace through the blood of his cross, by him to reconcile all things unto himself; by him, I say, whether they be things in earth, or things in heaven. And you, that were sometime alienated and enemies in your mind by wicked works, yet now hath he reconciled in the body of his flesh through death, to present you holy and unblameable and unreproveable in his sight" (Col. 1:20-22).

We are not to be influenced by our feelings and our condition, but rather by His written Word. In spiritual growth, the eye of faith is slowly transferred from our own point of view to His, from condition to position. By means of intelligent faith in the scriptural facts, we are to turn boldly from sinful darkness to rest in His holy light. "The entrance of thy words giveth light . . ." (Ps. 119:130). "But now in Christ Jesus ye who sometimes were far off are made nigh [reconciled to His presence] by the blood of Christ. For he is our peace . . ." (Eph. 2:13, 14). "For he hath made him to be sin for us, who knew no sin; that we might be made the righteousness of God in him" (2 Cor. 5:21). Since we are born into Christ, who is our righteousness, our Father is able to accept us fully into His presence, just as we are. Our right to the light is our eternal position, in spite of our present condition.

Our walk is the result of the source of our life. If we attempt to walk as Christians in dependence upon our own resources, there is self-centeredness, self-righteousness, and darkness. But when we walk in dependence upon the Source of our life in the light of God's presence, there is Christ-centeredness, His righteousness, and "the Lord shall be thine everlasting light" (Isa. 60:20).

The Principle of Position

In our estimation, which is looming larger, our sins, or His blood shed for those sins? Are we viewing our sins from His side, or ours? Are we letting God be God in this matter? It is for us to think God's thoughts after Him. He has graciously and justly placed us in His Son, the very Light of earth and heaven. Can our sins come between our Father and His glorified Son who is our life? Never! He has borne them all in His own body on the tree. He is our risen Advocate, Jesus Christ the righteous. By means of His atoning blood, He maintains eternally our relationship with the Father in unbroken integrity.

Though our sins can in no way affect our position in the light, or alter His thoughts of love toward us, they can and do affect *our* thoughts and attitude toward our Father. They can never cloud His view of our Advocate, but they can and do obliterate *our* vision of His advocacy. They immediately hinder our communion and fellowship with the Father and the Son. The dark cloud of guilt and conviction of sin settles down upon our heart and conscience, unless we learn to judge ourselves and willingly confess our sins before God. "For if we would judge ourselves, we should not be judged" (1 Cor. 11:31).

Chapter Ten

SINS AND CONFESSION

"If we confess our sins, he is faithful and just to forgive us our sins, and to cleanse us from all unrighteousness" (1 John 1:9). God the Father is free to forgive our sins because the Lord Jesus has already dealt with their source, the principle of sin. He condemned it in His flesh on the cross (Rom. 8:3). Confessing our sins, therefore, has nothing to do with condemnation, but with cleansing and communion.

CONDITION

The believer who is not aware of his perfect position before God, who does not realize that the Father has already placed him in the light of His presence, is more aware of his self-centered condition than his Christ-centered position. Hence he does not actually accept the benefit of his position in the light when he does confess his sins. He does not *feel* forgiven and cleansed of all unrighteousness, and soon gives up confessing. Thereafter he flounders in darkness and guilt. This is the predicament of all too many believers today.

In the early days of their Christian life, most believers are

The Principle of Position

quite faithful in confessing their sins to the Father. But, because they are yet babes, there is very little scriptural knowledge of what God has done about the indwelling source of those sins, and before long there are more sins committed than confessed. This accumulation of unconfessed sins brings guilt to the conscience, and the believer finds himself out of fellowship with the Father. Not only that, but he is experiencing chastisement. To make matters worse, he now seeks to hide from the light. He forgets that the purpose of light is not to punish and condemn the sinner, but to reveal sins so that they may be confessed and freely forgiven.

Another common error is that of praying for forgiveness, instead of heeding the Word, confessing the sins, and receiving the assurance of forgiveness. One may pray for forgiveness for months, and still not receive the assurance of it. Many admit sin in general, instead of confessing sins in particular. Assurance of forgiveness and cleansing are the sure result of honest and specific confession of sins committed in thought, word, or deed. There may be repentance and brokenness, but this is the result of confession and cleansing, not the cause. "If any man sin," there is immediate recourse to confession, and to Christ's advocacy and shed blood for complete forgiveness and cleansing. "If we *confess* our sins, he is faithful and just to forgive . . ." (1 John 1:9).

POSITION

When we rest in our position in Christ, we find that we are in the light. We know that our sins have been purged once for all and therefore our conscience is cleansed. At the same time, we are very much aware that although we abide in the risen Lord Jesus, our everyday Christian life is carried on in a sinful world. There are sins committed as we grow, because we take our eyes off the Lord Jesus and foolishly rely upon self; a defiled conscience and broken fellowship are the result. We also know that

Sins and Confession

the remedy is to confess our sins, thereby to receive cleansing from all unrighteousness and restoration of a clear conscience and blessed fellowship.

Our present experience is greatly inferior to our eternal position, no matter what the stage of our spiritual growth. The development of our condition is *toward* our finished position, and at the same time *from* that completed source. The discrepancy between our position and our condition, manifested by our many failures in growth and service, is justly taken care of by means of our confession and His cleansing. Our need is further met by Christ's faithful advocacy, whereby our position and fellowship are maintained throughout the progress of our spiritual growth. By these means our Lord ever keeps us dependent upon Himself, and at the same time fully confident in Him. Needy, but bold.

Abiding and walking in the light keeps us honestly aware of our sins, while also enhancing our appreciation of His grace. The realization of our sins does not cripple us, because His cleansing frees us. The light that reveals our sins manifests the Son, enabling us honestly to face both without fear. Where we are most detected, there we are most protected. Upon this basis, the sins that are committed are immediately dealt with, and we are able to continue in fellowship and growth. The only alternative is self-confidently to struggle with sin, to fail, and thereby to be hindered in our development.

Our Father's counter-action is the ministry of the indwelling Spirit of life. To have our sins so freely forgiven does not make us lax as to our walk. For one thing, with the forgiveness there is often His faithful chastisement. A good conscience is cherished too much for it to be lost by license. We admit that "we all often stumble and fall and offend in many things" (James 3:2, Amp.), but there need be no fear of facing up to each offence and confessing it. The light that reveals our sins ever reveals our perfect position in the Lord Jesus. For us, "the darkness is past, and the true light now shineth" (1 John 2:8).

Confession and cleansing enable us to rest before God without guile. Our attitude becomes, "Search me, O God, and know my heart: try me, and know my thoughts: and see if there be any wicked way in me . . ." (Ps. 139:23, 24). There is no pretension of being without sins; rather, we want them clearly revealed so that they may be confessed and thereby kept from breaking our all-important fellowship with the Father. We are faithfully taught the lesson not to attempt to hide our sins and refrain from confession. "When I kept silent about my sin, my body wasted away through my groaning all day long. For day and night Thy hand was heavy upon me . . ." (Ps. 32:3, 4, NASB). Guilt and chastisement do their thorough work, and we learn to appreciate the fact that God's way of confession is imperative.

All because of our position in the Lord Jesus, and in spite of our condition in ourselves, our Father is able to say to us, "For I know the thoughts that I think toward you . . . thoughts of peace, and not of evil, to give you an expected end" (Jer. 29:11). "Blessed is he whose transgression is forgiven, whose sin is covered. Blessed is the man unto whom the Lord imputeth not iniquity, and in whose spirit there is no guile" (Ps. 32:1, 2). "Therefore being justified by faith, we have peace with God through our Lord Jesus Christ: by whom also we have *access by faith into this grace wherein we stand,* and rejoice in hope of the glory of God" (Rom. 5:1, 2, italics mine).

As we grow, we learn to stand in our standing of grace, abiding in the risen Lord Jesus, and walking in the light of the Father's presence and fellowship. We appreciate the fact of our position as we experience failures in fighting against sin. We express our growing hatred of self by freely confessing our sins, which amounts to judging ourselves for submitting to indwelling sin. We admit our responsibility for walking (or drifting) beyond the realm of light, into the shadows of sin and self. "For if we would judge ourselves, we should not be judged. But when we are judged, we are chastened of the Lord, that we should not be condemned with the world" (1 Cor. 11:31, 32).

Standing in the light, we are not only aware that our sins have been cleared away by the blood, but we realize that we as sinners have also been put away by the death of the cross. We count ourselves to have died unto sin, and now to be alive as new creations in Christ Jesus. As such, we confess our sins as they are revealed in the light, and we are thereby made free from self-occupation—free to be fully occupied in fellowship with the Father and the Son.

To turn from the darkness and death of self to the light and life of Christ is not to give up the fight and give in to sin. Not at all! It is fighting "the good fight of *faith*" (1 Tim. 6:12), it is entering into the benefits of the fact that the fight has already been fought and won for us by Another. This transition from bondage and defeat to freedom and victory is the faith-move from condition to position. "For he that is entered into his rest, he also hath ceased from his own works, as God did from him" (Heb. 4:10).

The Holy Spirit brings us through this transition by a very simple process. He allows us to struggle with sin and self until we learn the futility of it. Then it is that He shows us that the Lord Jesus has already done for us what we can never do. It is from "O wretched man that I am! who shall deliver me from the body of this death?" to, "I thank God [He has already accomplished it] through Jesus Christ our Lord . . ." (Rom. 7:24, 25). It is from the bondage of the "law in my members, warring against the law of my mind, and bringing me into captivity to the law of sin which is in my members," to the liberty of "the law of the Spirit of life in Christ Jesus [which] hath made me free from the law of sin and death" (Rom. 7:23; 8:2).

Fellowship

"God is faithful, by whom ye were called unto the fellowship of His Son Jesus Christ our Lord" (1 Cor. 1:9). The root word for

The Principle of Position

fellowship and communion is *common*. Our communion with the Father and the Son, having fellowship one with another, is to have common thoughts, affections, and purposes. It is a oneness of heart and mind. It is to "love the Lord thy God with all thy heart . . . and with all thy mind . . ." (Luke 10:27). As we study His Word in dependence upon His Spirit, we are in communion with His thoughts. As we love the Lord Jesus, we are loving the One whom the Father loves with all His heart.

Free from self-condemnation, free from a guilty conscience, free in the faithful advocacy of the Lord Jesus, free in the confession of our sins and cleansing from all unrighteousness, we are in the light of His presence to worship Him, commune with Him, and grow in Him. "But we all, with open face beholding as in a glass the glory of the Lord, are changed into the same image from glory to glory, even as by the Spirit of the Lord" (2 Cor. 3:18). It is the look that justifies, but it is the gaze that sanctifies.

Having died in Christ to sin, Satan, law, and the world, we are freed and born anew, made new creations in the Lord Jesus. Abiding in Him in the light of the Father, we are at liberty to gaze upon Him in the full love of hearts and minds that are free from the palling darkness of unconfessed sins and a defiled conscience. No nervous, anxious or restless self-effort; just quiet rest in Him, knowing that our "life is hid with Christ in God" (Col. 3:3). By the ministry of the Spirit of Christ within, the life of the Lord Jesus is manifested increasingly in our everyday walk.

Our Father's purpose for us is that we become conformed to the image (character) of His Son. To that end, all things are being "worked together" (Rom. 8:28,29). In our position in Christ, our Father has already perfected us, made us complete in Him. In our walk, He by His Spirit is fashioning us after that blessed pattern, "that the life also of Jesus might be made manifest in our mortal flesh" (2 Cor. 4:11).

"He that saith he abideth in him ought himself also so to walk, even as he walked" (1 John 2:6). In the first place, the Lord Jesus walked in the light, in fellowship with His Father. ". . . The Son of man which is in heaven" (John 3:13). Secondly, He walked in full dependence upon the Holy Spirit. "Then was Jesus led up of the Spirit into the wilderness . . ." (Matt. 4:1). ". . . Who through the eternal Spirit offered Himself without spot to God . . ." (Heb. 9:14). Likewise, our life is hid with Christ in God, and we walk in the light of God's presence during our earthly course. Our dependence is expressed as we "walk in the Spirit," that we may not "fulfil the lust of the flesh" (Gal. 5:16). We are to ". . . worship in the Spirit of God and glory in Christ Jesus and put no confidence in the flesh" (Phil. 3:3, NASB).

One of the Father's means of teaching us the Spirit-dependent walk in the light is to let us flounder in the darkness of self. The Lord Jesus also patiently waits to show us that all our sins have been cleansed by His blood. Coupled with our sins is the crushing weight of an evil conscience, which is often endured for years. And He continues to wait for us to acknowledge our position in Him in the light, so that we may rest in what He has already done about our sins. "Let us draw near with a sincere heart in full assurance of faith, having our hearts sprinkled clean from an evil conscience . . ." (Heb. 10:22, NASB).

"How much more shall the blood of Christ, who through the eternal Spirit offered himself without spot to God, purge your conscience from dead works to serve the living God?" (Heb. 9:14). Laboring under a load of unconfessed sins, we are disqualified from fellowship with our Father, as well as from usefulness to others; we are, rather, a burden to all. It is such believers whom He urges to "come boldly unto the throne of grace, that we may obtain mercy, and find grace to help in time of need" (Heb. 4:16). The need is ever present, the work is forever done! He has placed us in His Son, having "made us sit together in heavenly places in Christ Jesus" (Eph. 2:6). All that is required is that we confidently abide where we have already been placed.

The Principle of Position

We are not to abide in our present condition, counting upon help from Him in heaven for our walk and service. Just the opposite! He has shown us our position in order that we may abide in our risen Lord, in the light and presence of the Father. It is from that vantage point that we become involved in the needs of this world. In John 3:13 our Lord Jesus referred to Himself as "he that came down from heaven, even the Son of man which is in heaven." He shared heavenly life in a world of need. If He is to do the same and more today, through us, we must abide in heaven as we sojourn on earth. Only life lived in the light of glory can overcome the world of darkness.

In summary, (1) we count ourselves to have died unto sin, and to be alive unto God in the Lord Jesus (Rom. 6:11); (2) we accept our position in the light when we know ourselves to be new creations in our risen Savior (Eph. 2:6); (3) we enjoy His blessed fellowship as we judge ourselves in confession of our sins (1 John 1:7, 9). Then it is that our Lord can work through us in the lives of others, "to open their eyes, and to turn them from darkness to light, and from the power of Satan unto God, that they may receive forgiveness of sins, and inheritance among them which are sanctified by faith that is in me" (Acts 26:18).

Keep Looking Down

"For you have died and your life is hidden with Christ in God" (Col. 3:3, NASB).